APOSTASY

A Study in the Epistle to the Hebrews
and in Baptist History

"Take care, brethren, lest there be in any of you an evil, unbelieving heart, leading you to fall away (*apostēnai* in Greek) from the living God. But exhort one another every day, as long as it is called 'today,' that none of you may be hardened by the deceitfulness of sin. For we share in Christ, if only we hold our first confidence firm to the end" (Hebrews 3:12-14, RSV).

"I appeal to you, brethren, bear with my word of exhortation, for I have written to you briefly" (Hebrews 13:22, RSV).

APOSTASY

A Study in the Epistle to the Hebrews
and in Baptist History

by
Dale Moody

Emeritus Professor of Christian Theology
Southern Baptist Theological Seminary
Louisville, Kentucky

SMYTH & HELWYS PUBLISHING, INC.
Greenville, South Carolina

APOSTASY

A Study in the Epistle to the Hebrews
and in Baptist History

International Standard Book Number 0-9628455-3-1

This book is produced using acid-free paper exceeding the minimum standards set by the National Historical Publications and Records Commission.

Smyth & Helwys Publishing, Inc.
P. O. Box 72
Greenville, South Carolina 29602

Dedicated to the Memory

of

John Smyth (d. 1612)
Thomas Helwys (c.1570 - c.1615)
Thomas Grantham (c.1634 - 1692)

———————

a theological trio among British Baptists
with whom the author finds
broad agreement and spiritual kinship

Table of Contents

Preface

I am grateful to the new publishing company of Smyth & Helwys for their willingness to publish this biblical and historical study which is basic in Baptist theology. This basic New Testament doctrine is now in the very eye of what is called "the controversy" among Southern Baptists. The lectures that follow were first written in 1990 for the Trinity Baptist Church (Progressive Baptist) of Baltimore, Maryland where my very dear friend Dr. William C. Calhoun is pastor. He even invited me back later this year.

Later also, September 14-15, the last three chapters were repeated as the Northern Tier Bible Lectureship at the Minot Christian Church in Minot, North Dakota. There Evangelist Rowlie Hutton endeared himself to me not only for the invitation but for the warm friendship behind the plastic plague that declared me a true "Buckeye Baptist."

The term "Buckeye Baptist" I first applied to Walter Scott, the first great evangelist of the movement that became the quest for "the ancient order of things." Today another "Campbellite" friend, Leroy Garrett of Denton, Texas, has described in scholarly detail what he now calls The Stone Campbell Movement (College Press, 1981).

It was also in 1981 that the first edition of my summary of Christian doctrine, *The Word of Truth* (Wm. B. Eerdmans Publishing Company, 1981, 1990), stirred up a theological "desert storm" with Chapter 55 on "Apostasy." May showers of blessing follow.

Numerous people have requested this short statement for use and distribution. I should thank especially Ollie Latch, a long time friend and a leader among the General Baptists of Popular Bluff, Missouri, for his eagerness to get this in print. He is most certainly right in seeing a parallel in Benoni Stinson (1798-1869) with whom I am flattered to be compared.

There are so many others to thank, but this must finally go to press.

Dale Moody, "Little Rapids"
Box 1865
Louisville, Kentucky 40280
January 16, 1991

Introduction
A Very Personal Word

This study goes back to 1941 when I was pastor of Calvary Baptist Church in Mexia, Texas. I preached through the Epistle to the Hebrews with the help of A. T. Robertson's *Word Pictures in the New Testament* (Sunday School Board of the Southern Baptist Convention, 1934). I agreed with Robertson's interpretation of the passages that I now call the Five Exhortations. As I remember I went beyond Robertson on the question of authorship only.

It so happened that Welch Sewell, beloved Chairman of the Deacons at Calvary Baptist Church often reported my sermons in the *Mexia Daily News*, so I had readers in a large area, especially in the Limestone Baptist Association. At the end of the summer I returned to Louisville to begin my studies for the Th.D. degree as the last graduate student under the now immortal W. O. Carver. Dr. Carver had sent me back to Baylor University to complete my hours, all in Latin and German, for the B. A. degree (cum laude), "if I ever expected to teach at Southern Baptist Theological Seminary."

This word got out among preachers in the Limestone Baptist Association. First, the Moderator wrote Dr. John R. Sampey warning him that I did not seem to agree with the landmark doctrine of "Eternal Security," a term J. M. Carroll, brother of B. H. Carroll, had borrowed from the very popular book on salvation by L. S.

1

Chafer (Sunday School Times, 1917). Dr. Chafer was President and Professor of Systematic Theology at Dallas Theological Seminary. I had two courses in theology under Chafer. I left Dallas in 1937 and became a student in Louisville. Even though Dr. Chafer gave me the grade of 100 in both his courses in Systematic Theology, I did not agree with him on several issues, especially Eternal Security and what he called True Evangelism in which he refused to make evangelistic invitations and to practice water baptism.

In his Dispensationalism Dr. Chafer claimed that water baptism was for the Fifth Dispensation and that "Spirit baptism" was for the Sixth Dispensation. Since Dallas required agreement with Chafer's theology of all students for matriculation and graduation, I left for Louisville where I would be free to preach and practice all of the New Testament. This freedom I enjoyed until 1984 when my thirty seven years of teaching were terminated over the issue of Eternal Security or Security of the Believer, as J. R. Graves taught in the nineteenth century.

I resisted all creedalism that required me to reject the supreme authority of the Scriptures, especially Article XIII of the Seminary Abstract of Principles of 1858 which not only contradicted verbally Hebrews 6:4-6 but also contradicted Articles I and XVIII of the Abstract of Principles. This was brought forth out of obscurity and used against me.

The Moderator of the Limestone Baptist Association called himself the "Kosse Parson" in his articles in the *Mexia Daily News*. He first of all had Dr. J. B. Tidwell of Baylor University to preach the Limestone Baptist Association annual sermon against my interpretation. Then he wrote a letter to Dr. John R. Sampey with a

clipping about my views from the *Mexia Daily News.* All
of this is thoroughly documented by Clark Youngblood
in his doctoral dissertation at Southern Baptist Theological Seminary.

Dr. John R. Sampey said nothing to me of this
correspondence until our dear friend and his student
counselor, Dr. Hugh R. Peterson, told me that "Old
Tig," as we called Dr. Sampey, had received the letter. I
went immediately to Dr. Sampey. A very long conver-
sation which followed concluded with Dr. Sampey
pounding his desk about "those rascals who thought
that they could just make a profession of faith and then
live like the Devil." When I told Dr. Sampey I taught
exactly what A. T. Robertson had said in his *Word Pictures*, which was true, he warmly assured me that I
would not go wrong following Robertson. "I would
trust Robertson with my soul," he said. I told him I
would not go that far, but that I did then as I do now,
think Robertson was usually right in his interpretations
on the Greek New Testament.

When Dr. Ellis Fuller, Dr. Sampey's successor, later
asked me to become a faculty member and sign the
"Abstract of Principles" required of all teachers, I told
him the Sampey story and pointed out the contradiction
between Article XIII of the "Abstract" and Hebrews 6:4-
6. Dr. Fuller assured me that any persons that agreed
with his beloved teacher Robertson had a right to teach
in Southern Seminary.

I told him at that time that President Henry P. Van
Dusen of Union Theological Seminary in the City of
New York wanted to recommend me to Colgate-Roches-
ter Seminary and bring me back later to teach at Union.
Of course, I loved Southern and Southern Baptists and
wanted to stay in Louisville, my wife's home. That I did

for thirty nine years. Until 1961 I labored with the tension between articles I and XVIII on the authority of the Scriptures and the contradiction of the Scriptures in Article XIII which I had traced back to the Elder William Collins of Petty France Baptist Church in London. In 1677 he had made this error as he worked over the Westminster Confession of Faith of 1646-48 by Presbyterians and presented it as the Second London Confession of Faith for Baptists. I have not yet found a Southern Baptist scholar who denies this contradiction. I thought then and I think now it should be dropped as the Baptist Faith and Message of 1963 did.

From my study of all the Baptist confessions in history I then found and still do find the Standard Confession of the General Baptists in 1660 nearest to the Scriptures. All my Baptist friends declared that the Scriptures were "the only source" as Article I of the Abstract declared. That is still true.

When I said that was my position at a pastors' conference at the University Baptist Church in Shawnee, Oklahoma in 1961, a controversy followed. One brother said that what I believed might be "Bible" but it was not "Baptist." I insisted it was then Baptists that need to change, not the Bible; I was surprised at the strong support I got, especially from students at Oklahoma Baptist University across the street. Most of them had learned Greek well under a good teacher at O.B.U.; however, a minority would not let the issue rest at that. Sam Scantlan, who had invited me to the conference, later went before the Oklahoma City pastors and got them to pass a resolution against me. He was the only one among the Oklahoma city pastors who had heard my discussion in Shawnee.

Twenty years later there was almost a repetition of

this conflict between Scripture and a Baptist cliché in the North Little Rock Baptist Church in Arkansas. Most of what follows as the Fourth Exhortation is verbatim what I said. David Miller, Director of Missions in the Little Red River Baptist Association, responded in fury, even though I got a standing ovation from most. Two days later at the Arkansas Baptist Convention, after I had returned to Louisville, Miller had rallied his support and got the group to pass a resolution against me. At the close of my message I offered my manuscript for publication and would welcome any response to my views. Thus far I have seen none.

The expositions that follow have been delivered many times and some parts have been previously printed. They are offered now in print at the request of many. I am willing to make any further response requested that all may be built up in mature Christian life and thought.

The careful and mature scholar will discover little new in my interpretation. In 1962 I was telling the late F. F. Bruce about my Oklahoma ordeal. He responded by saying he would soon publish his exposition of Hebrews which would vindicate most that I had said. In 1964 his book was published and he did, indeed, give support. In fact, I would today suggest his 1990 revision and expansion as the best exposition of Hebrews thus far.

Many will also be surprised to find both the Reformed Scholar, Simon J. Kistemaker (*Expositions of the Epistle to the Hebrews*, Baker, 1985) and the Roman Catholic, Harold Attridge (*Hebrews*, Fortress, 1989) singing the same tune as I do. The commentaries by P. E. Hughes (Eerdmans, 1977) and Donald Hagner (Harper, 1985) are near satisfaction, but they show some lack of courage at a few points. Calvinistic constraint takes over especially when they get to the notorious Hebrews 6:4-6. Other writers of importance appear in my exposition and application. I look forward to reading the forthcoming commentaries by William L. Lane in the Word Biblical Commentary (Word, forthcoming) and by Bruce Corley in the New American Commentary (Broadman Press, forthcoming). Any valid correction of my views will be welcome.

In his book *Once Saved, Always Saved* (Hodder and Stoughton, 1983; Moody Press, 1985), R. T. Kendall finally concludes "that Hebrews 6:4-6 describes saved people who could not be renewed again unto repentance" (p. 221). Surely he does not mean to say that one can "crucify the Son of God a fresh" and be without "repentance" and still be eternally secure in his salvation. This is at least far from what L. S. Chafer in 1917 meant by "Eternal Security."

In his book, *Eternal Security* (Nelson, 1990), Charles Stanley concedes that those exhorted had "originally been converted" (p. 146) or "who have believed" (p. 148), but he believes this is "a unique situation" because they are Jewish believers who are tempted to renounce Christianity and return to Judaism. Is God easier on Jews than he is on Gentiles? As Stanley says on page 147, "Think about it!"

The First Exhortation
Hebrews 2:1-4

> Therefore we must pay the closer attention to
> what we have heard, lest we drift away from it. For if
> the message declared by angels was valid and every
> transgression or disobedience received a just retribu-
> tion, how shall we escape if we neglect such a great
> salvation? It was declared at first by the Lord, and it
> was attested to us by those who heard him, while
> God also bore witness by signs and wonders and
> various miracles and by gifts of the Holy Spirit dis-
> tributed according to his own will.

According to Tertullian of Carthage (c. 160-c. 225),
the first Latin Father, the so-called Epistle to the Hebrews was written by Barnabas. He seems to have no
doubt about this authorship when he quotes Hebrews in
his writing on modesty (*De pudicitia*, 20). There is no
early evidence to the contrary.

According to Luke, in his second summary about
the common life among the disciples of Jesus in the
church of Jerusalem, there was a generous and liberal
man named Joseph Barnabas. Luke's second summary
says:

> Now the company of those who believed were of
> one heart and soul, and no one said that any of the
> things which he possessed was his own, but they had
> everything in common. And with great power the
> apostles gave their testimony to the resurrection of
> the Lord Jesus, and great grace was upon them all.
> There was not a needy person among them, for as
> many as were possessors of lands or houses sold

7

them, and brought the proceeds of what was sold and
laid it at the apostles' feet; and distribution was made
to each as any had need. Thus Joseph who was sur-
named by the apostles Barnabas (which means, Son of
encouragement), a Levite, a native of Cyprus, sold a
field which belonged to him, and brought the money
and laid it at the apostles' feet. (Acts 4:32-37)

The lying hypocrisy of Ananias and his wife
Sapphira stood in vivid contrast.

But a man named Ananias with his wife Sapphira
sold a piece of property, and with his wife's knowledge he kept back some of the proceeds, and brought
only a part and laid it at the apostles' feet. But Peter
said, "Ananias, why has Satan filled your heart to lie
to the Holy Spirit and to keep back part of the proceeds of the land? While it remained unsold, did it
not remain your own? And after it was sold, was it
not at your disposal? How is it that you have con-
trived this deed in your heart? You have not lied to
men but to God." When Ananias heard these words,
he fell down and died. And great fear came upon all
who heard of it. The young men rose and wrapped
him up and carried him out and buried him. (Acts
5:1-6)

If this Joseph Barnabas is the author of Hebrews
then the concluding exhortations in Hebrews 13 are
greatly illuminated.

Let brotherly love continue. Do not neglect to
show hospitality to strangers, for thereby some have
entertained angels unawares. Remember those who
are in prison, as though in prison with them; and
those who are ill-treated, since you also are in the
body. Let marriage be held in honor among all, and
let the marriage bed be undefiled; for God will judge
the immoral and adulterous. Keep your life free from

love of money, and be content with what you have; for he has said, "I will never fail you nor forsake you." Hence we can confidently say,

"The Lord is my helper, I will not be afraid; what can man do to me?"

Remember your leaders, those who spoke to you the word of God; consider the outcome of their life, and imitate their faith. Jesus Christ is the same yesterday and today and for ever. Do not be led away by diverse and strange teachings; for it is well that the heart be strengthened by grace, not by foods, which have not benefited their adherents. We have an altar from which those who serve the tent have no right to eat. For the bodies of those animals whose blood is brought into the sanctuary by the high priest as a sacrifice for sin are burned outside the camp. So Jesus also suffered outside the gate in order to sanctify the people through his own blood. Therefore let us go forth to him outside the camp and bear the abuse he endured. For here we have no lasting city, but we seek the city which is to come. Through him then let us continually offer up a sacrifice of praise to God, that is, the fruit of lips that acknowledge his name. Do not neglect to do good and to share what you have, for such sacrifices are pleasing to God.

Obey your leaders and submit to them; for they are keeping watch over your souls, as men who will have to give account. Let them do this joyfully, and not sadly, for that would be of no advantage to you.

Pray for us, for we are sure that we have a clear conscience, desiring to act honorably in all things. I urge you the more earnestly to do this in order that I may be restored to you the sooner.

Now may the God of peace who brought again from the dead our Lord Jesus, the great shepherd of the sheep, by the blood of the eternal covenant equip you with everything good that you may do his will, working in you that which is pleasing in his sight, through Jesus Christ; to whom be glory for ever and ever. Amen.

This seems to be a clear picture of the situation in Jerusalem or Caesarea or Antioch or even Cyrene from which Barnabas wrote and among Jewish believers in Rome who first read this Epistle soon after the playboy Emperor Nero committed suicide in A.D. 68 and just before the fall of the Temple in Jerusalem in A.D. 70. This would be just one generation of forty years between the crucifixion of Jesus and the writing of what Joseph Barnabas calls "my word of exhortation." This seems to be a reference to his Greek name meaning "Son of exhortation."

The first readers are exhorted to "pay the closer attention to what we have heard, lest we drift away from it" (2:1). It is rather obvious at first reading that "we" in "we have heard," "we drift," and "we neglect" means the one who writes and those who read. However, some who do not wish to face this danger pounce upon the "we drift" (*pararuomen*, the passive of *pararreō*) to argue that the danger is that God may flow by us and leave us standing on the bank (H. H. Hobbs, *The Epistle to the Hebrews*, Convention Press, 1951, p. 37). I prefer to follow the interpretation of A. T. Robertson who agrees with all the other interpreters I know that the passive of *pararreō*, "to flow," would be "drift." This interpretation does not pacify the advocates of so-called "eternal security," a view that seems to go back to Lewis Sperry Chafer's widely used book, *Salvation* (Philadelphia: Sunday School Times, 1917; especially chapters X and XI, pp. 96-137).

This was made popular among Southern Baptists by J. M. Carroll's sermon on "The Eternal Security of the Blood-Bought Believer" when he preached as a pulpit guest of Clarence Walker at the Ashland Avenue Baptist Church in Lexington, Kentucky. When I advocated the view of A. T. Robertson and all the other scholarly interpreters I know, that sermon by J. M. Carroll was put back into circulation by John R. Rice in his paper called *The Sword of the Lord* (July 26, 1963). Baptists in Oklahoma were calling for my termination as a professor at Southern Baptist Theological Seminary in Louisville, Kentucky, so John R. Rice was trying to add fuel to the fire.

My book, *The Word of Truth*, (Eerdmans, 1981, 1990) gives more details, but no scholarly interpretation from F. F. Bruce's good defense in 1964 to the present has refuted my exegesis or exposed any historical errors. An abundance of scholarly writing, including recent works by Harold Attridge (Fortress Press, 1989) and William L. Lane (Word, 1991), supports my view.

A second scholarly debate is focused on Hebrews 2:2. Joseph Barnabas follows the belief also in Acts 7:53 and Galatians 3:19, based on the Septuagint translation of Deuteronomy 33:2, that the law of Moses was mediated by angels. His appeal from the lesser to the greater is that if every transgression or disobedience of the law of Moses received "a just retribution of disobedience" another question is raised about the superior revelation in the gospel of Jesus and the apostles "while God bore witness by signs and wonders and various miracles and gifts of the Holy Spirit distributed according to his will" (2:4). The question is, "how shall we escape if we neglect so great a salvation" (2:3)?

This general view in this briefest of the five exhortations in Hebrews has been greatly clarified by two background studies. The first is a study of the background on "every transgression and disobedience which received a just retribution." In my background reading the doctoral dissertation by George Coates, now of the

Lexington Theological Seminary, written under the great Walter Zimmerli of the University of Goettingen, Germany, is a major help. The book by George Coates was called *Rebellion in the Wilderness* (Abingdon, 1968). His study of a source about seven great rebellions in the Jewish Torah has been utilized by Philip J. Budd in his illuminating commentary on Numbers in the Word Biblical Commentary, 1984. To the scholarly I recommend these two books which are the background to my less scholarly use of the seven rebellions.

The first of these rebellions may be called the Golden Calf Rebellion found by itself in Exodus 32:1-35. This belongs to the oldest written source on the Jewish Torah. When Moses returns from his forty day vigil with the Lord at the top of Sinai he finds his brother Aaron leading the Israelites in the worship of the Golden Calf with the claim that it was not Yahweh who gave the "ten words" to Moses who brought them out of Egypt but the Golden Calf, the fertility symbol which was later to become the transgression of the Northern Kingdom (cf. Israel under Jeroboam I, 1 Kings 12).

Moses is so perturbed that his intercessory prayer asks the Lord to forgive the people even if it requires the name of Moses to be blotted out of the book of life (Ex 32:32). This the Lord would not do, but he said that he would blot out the names of all the people who had done this great sin (Ex 32:33).

Once when I was teaching Exodus in a large church, a Director of Missions, our word for a Baptist bishop, exploded that he had always heard that a name could never be blotted out. Time and time I had heard the same popular dodge (cf. the clear teaching of the text here and a half dozen other places in the Bible), but when I told this important official to debate the issue

with the Lord who said it, not me, he pouted for the rest
of the service, and I am not sure he has forgiven me yet.
He seemed to think Exodus 32:33 should vanish from
his Bible because his oral tradition said otherwise. This
illustrates the power of oral tradition, often over the
clear statement of Scripture. It is no wonder that Jesus
later, speaking on another problem, said: "You leave
the commandment of God, and hold fast to the tradi-
tions of men" (Mark 7:8).

A second example may be called the Fleshpot
Rebellion (Ex 16:3; Num 11:1-35). The recipe for the
fleshpot of "the cucumber, the melons, the leeks, the
onions and the garlic" with the Nile River perch in
Egypt is given in Exodus 16:3. I can testify from experience that it was and still is good, but it became the
symbol of the rebellion of the Israelites as they tired of
manna even with occasional quail. The guides of the
Sinai show what they still call "the graves of craving"
now, but this murmuring remained the synonym for
rebellion even in Paul (1 Cor 10:1-13; Phil 2:14-18) and
the Gospel of John (6:22-71).

A third rebellion may be called the Big Sister Rebellion (Num 12:1-16). Big sister Miriam not only found
fault with the Cushite wife Moses had married but she
also raised the question: "Has the Lord indeed spoken
only to Moses? Has he not spoken through us also?"
That was not only sibling rivalry between big sister
Miriam and little brother Moses, but it was "woman's
lib" at its worst. For that rebellion Miriam was smitten
with leprosy. Even when she repented and was healed
she was "shut up outside the camp seven days" before
she was "brought in again" (Num 12:14).

The fourth and most famous rebellion may be called
the Grasshopper Rebellion (Num 13, 14). All but two,

Joshua and Caleb, brought back an evil report when the twelve spies returned from an intelligence invasion of Canaan. Ten of them said they felt like grasshoppers when they saw the tall giants and walls in the Promised Land. More than any it was Caleb who believed they could take the land with the help of the Lord. Those with the grasshopper complex were doomed to die in the wilderness with all who were of military age when they left Egypt.

The fifth great transgression and disobedience was Korah's Earthquake Rebellion against Moses and Aaron (Num 16). Korah also was of Levitical descent, so he led a takeover against the Aaronic priesthood. It reminds one of the fundamentalist conservatives and the moderate conservatives in the Southern Baptist Convention meeting in Phoenix near the Grand Canyon. Indeed, the Sinai guides today point out how the great canyon of Maktesh Ramon meets many of the features of Korah's Rebellion. A Jewish story says that you can hear the murmuring of Korah's followers if you put your ear to the ground at the supposed place where the 250 rebellious Levites were swallowed up in Sheol (Num 16:30). The story goes that those in Sheol are murmuring still: "Moses was right!" Be that as it may, Moses warned before the earthquake: "You have gone too far" (Num 16:3, 7).

The sixth story was the Serpent Rebellion made famous by the Gospel of John which says: "As Moses lifted up the serpent in the wilderness, even so must the Son of man be lifted up, that whosoever believes in him may have eternal life" (3:14f.).

It is not easy to discover what connection John saw between the death of Jesus and the Golden Serpent in the wilderness, but the account in Numbers 21:4-9 did.

I have actually seen images of a bronze serpent between Mount Hor and Ezion-geber near King Solomon's mines. The so-called Nehushtan was later a popular symbol of worship during the Israelite monarchy (2 Kings 18:4). I have been to a Buddhist snake temple in Malaysia. When they offered to make a photograph of me with a snake wrapped around my head I politely declined. I felt something like the reporter who visited a snake handling service in Appalachia. He went to the front with the preacher. At the appropriate moment a man came into the one room church, which had only a front door, and promptly took a snake out of his box and pitched it to another person with a "Hallelujah." This continued across the first pews and the reporter sensed that the snake would soon be up front, so he said to the snake handling preacher, "Where is your back door?" When told they did not have one, he politely asked, "Where would you like for me to make one?"

I note that the Church of Christ preachers who make so much over Mark 16:16 in the long ending of Mark never speak of the five signs that follow in 16:17-18. We all are a bit selective in our exegesis.

The seventh symbol of rebellion was at Baal Beth Peor when Israelite men and Moabite women were shacking up near Shittim in the bushes. This was a vital part of Baal worship. In Numbers 25:1-18 things get rather explicit when "Phinehas, the son of Eleazar, son of Aaron" followed an Israelite and found him in a sexual embrace with a Moabite woman and pinned them to the floor with a spear as he went after them into the inner room (25:6-8). The punishment by plague was twenty-four thousand. This is the only clear place in the Hebrew Scriptures where it is said that a human act "turned back" the wrath of God, although Zechariah 7:2, 8:22 and Malachi 1:9 have also been suggested by Leon Morris in his comments on Romans 3:25 (*The Cross in the New Testament*, Eerdmans, 1965). The Greek Scriptures has the idea in 1 Maccabees 3:8 and 2 Maccabees 7:38. This is important for understanding the proper emphasis on Hebrews 2:17.

A second background study needed for the understanding of this first exhortation is the meaning of salvation. Salvation in Hebrews is always an inheritance of the future (1:14). Therefore, those who neglect this salvation will not escape the judgment (2:3). Christ is the Pioneer or Leader (*archēgos*) of salvation because he himself was made perfect through suffering (2:10).

> In the days of his flesh, Jesus offered up prayers and supplications, with loud cries and tears, to him who was able to save him from death, and he was heard for his godly fear. Although he was a son, he learned obedience through what he suffered; and being made perfect he became the source of eternal salvation to all who obey him, being designated by God a high priest after the order of Melchizedek. (5:7-10)

Being "saved," having "learned" and "being made perfect" revealed in the incarnation the salvation waiting us when he "will appear a second time, not to deal with sin but for the salvation of those who are eagerly waiting for him" (9:28, cf. 6:9; 10:39). Hebrews can, therefore, use salvation to describe Noah's preparation of an ark for his household to come safely through the flood (11:7).

As there was no salvation for his household outside the ark, so there is no salvation outside Christ (cf.

1 Pet 3:18-22). A call for salvation is a call to get aboard the ark of salvation. That is why the church is often pictured as a ship and even the place for the worshipers in the meeting house of faith is called the "nave." Unless we stay aboard the ship we will not be saved. Although the author of Hebrews was perhaps Joseph Barnabas, the view of salvation is much the same as in Paul's epistles (1 Thess 5:8f.; 2 Thess 2:10; 3:15; 2 Cor 1:6; 6:2; 7:10; Rom 1:16; 10:1, 10; 11:11; 13:11; Phil 1:19, 29; 2:12; Eph 1:13; 2 Tim 2:10; 3:15). Those who glibly talk about "once-saved, always-saved," as if it is a past transaction so that now one cannot lose "his salvation" miss most of the meaning of salvation. A salvation that is solely in the past tense is a perversion of the New Testament meaning of salvation (see my book, *The Word of Truth,* especially chapter 49).

An elaboration on the witnesses to this great salvation in the first exhortation of Hebrews 2:1-4 would involve much that is said about Jesus as the Christ (*The Word of Truth,* Part VIII). That which was "declared at first by the Lord" and "attested to us by those who heard, while God also bore witness by signs and wonders and various miracles by gifts of the Holy Spirit distributed according to his will" is best summarized and expanded in the Four Gospels.

The Four Gospels
The Gospel of Mark (Word, 1988), by Robert A. Guelick of Fuller Theological Seminary, has now begun the most detailed summary of the many efforts to explore the treasures of the oldest source. He does not note the evidence for six different tractates, three with the Messianic Secret at the center (to 8:30) followed by

three with the Messianic Suffering introduced by the death of Jesus as a ransom (10:45) after three predictions of the Passion (8:31; 9:30-31; 10:33-34). This becomes the preface to the last week with the Passion narrative (14:1-18) that tells the story of the Son of God on earth. (See further the article by David E. Garland in the *Mercer Dictionary of the Bible*, 1990).

The Gospel of Matthew, now being expounded in two volumes by Donald A. Hagner, also of Fuller, promises also to do a critical and constructive update on the redaction criticism, stimulated by the creative discussion on Matthew's literary and theological art by Robert H. Gundry in his commentary on Matthew (Eerdmans, 1982). The devout need not fear that the foundations will be destroyed by any theological termites stirred up by this profound probing. Fuller must, indeed, be a good place to study the Gospels in these days.

From the beginning to the end Matthew is intended to equip Jewish disciples of Jesus as the Second Moses in Antioch on how to become a light to the Gentiles by using the Jewish Scriptures! (See especially the article by Ramsey Michaels on Matthew in the *Mercer Dictionary of the Bible*, 1990).

The Gospel of Luke is the fruit of this Gentile mission going forth from Caesarea in Palestine and reaching the capital of the Empire in Rome. This Gospel is concerned with the history of the great salvation against the background of the apocalyptic eschatology in Mark and Matthew. The prospects of the fall of Jerusalem within the generation of Jesus looms large in at least six predictions by Jesus of the event (Luke 11:29-32, 49-52; 13:34; 19:42-44; 21:20-24; 23:28-31). A personal eschatology of Hades (16:23) and Paradise

(23:43) supplements belief in salvation history. Luke does not negate the death of Jesus as a ransom in Mark (10:45), but he views the death of Jesus as that of a righteous man who forgives those who repent. Ransom and repentance have led to different views of atonement, but the two views can be harmonized. Prayer, possessions, and the place of women loom large in the teachings of Luke.

Debate about the date of Luke is very unstable, but one before the fall of Jerusalem in A. D. 70 is most satisfactory for me. I am unable to comprehend how Acts would say so much about Jerusalem with not a hint about its fall in A. D. 70 and end where it does with Luke written first if that event was in the past. John A. T. Robinson's *The Re-Dating of the New Testament* (Westminster, 1976) has not been taken seriously enough.

The Gospel of John is rightly praised by Clement of Alexandria as the "spiritual gospel." It has a dozen great passages on the Holy Spirit: six about the work of the Spirit in the ministry of Jesus and six about the Spirit in the life of the disciples.

The Gospel of John has been studied by the brightest and best interpreters of the Scriptures. Over a century ago B. F. Westcott, the major English personality in exploring the original Greek manuscripts, published his pioneer commentary of the Gospel of John. It greatly supplements his great commentary on Hebrews. Other English scholars such as C. H. Dodd (Cambridge, 1958), C. K. Barrett (Westminster, 1978), and Leon Morris (Eerdmans, 1971) have labored to throw more light on the Gospel of John.

In the significant revival of Biblical studies in Roman Catholicism such scholars as the German Rudolf Schnackenburg (Herder, 1968; Crossroad, 1982) and the

American R. E. Brown (Doubleday, 1966, 1970) have increased our knowledge of John.

Some Baptist scholars such as George Beasley-Murray (Word, 1987) and R. Alan Culpepper (Fortress, 1983) have been on the growing edge of Johannine studies.

The more than two year ministry in the Gospel of John does not displace the chronology of the Synoptic Gospels. Our understanding of the Christ Event is greatly enriched by the addition of the Logos doctrine. Details on the ministry of John the Baptist, the use of three Passovers and at least three other Jewish feasts, miracles in the Seven Signs, the Farewell Discourses added to the Paschal Mystery are major expansions in the Fourth Gospel. The two Rudolfs, Rudolf Bultmann, the Protestant, and Rudolf Schnackenburg, the Roman Catholic, should both be read for balance, but I find myself nearer to the late John A. T. Robinson in his challenging Bampton Lectures on *The Priority of the Fourth Gospel* (SCM Press, 1985). Every effort to drive a wedge between the "spiritual" John and "the sacramental" John I resist. John is theological history.

As Hebrews 2:3 and following is a brief statement of the Christ Event, so the Four Gospels are significant supplements to our understanding. As Tatian put them together in the second century, even so we should "harmonize" with them as a Gospel Choir in the twentieth century. This requires diligent study of the major contribution of the ancient Christian gospels. (See *Ancient Christian Gospels: Their History and Development* by Helmut Koester of Harvard University, Trinity Press International, 1990). Many may shrink back from the profound analysis, beginning with the publication of the Gospel of Thomas, of all the ancient Christian gospels, but I have long looked for such a study. Especially important is Tatian's *Diatessaron*, which was his attempt about 171 A.D. to create the one Gospel for the Church from the Four Gospels, (the meaning of the term *Diatessaron*). This is treated in the special study by William L. Peterson (Peeters, 1985).

The Second Exhortation

Hebrews 3:7-4:11

The major emphasis in this second exhortation in Hebrews comes to focus on the sinful condition called "hardness of heart." Hardness of heart in the Hebrew Scriptures finds a classic example in the Pharaoh of Egypt. Whether this Pharaoh was Amunhotep II, the son of Thutmose III of the 18th dynasty (as advocated by John Garstand and so fervently argued by my beloved teacher J. McKee Adams), or Rameses II, son of Seti I of the 19th dynasty (the majority opinion of the last generation), the Pharaoh of the Exodus became the chief symbol for hardness of heart as stubborn resistance and unforgivable resistance to the will of God. I am unable to resist the feeling that John Garstand, from whom I first learned most details, was basically correct in his learned study, *The Foundations of Biblical History* (University of Liverpool Press, 1931). Recent studies tend to confirm the date of the Exodus around 1446.

As a very small boy and as a young Texas Baptist preacher, I heard the great and good George W. Truett often quote what he called an old hymn about hardness of heart. His book of sermons called *A Quest for Souls* (Broadman Press, 1917, pp. 370f.) is the written source for my knowledge of the following words.

There is a time, I know not when,
  A place, I know not where,
Which marks the destiny of men
  To heaven or despair.
There is a line by us not seen,
  Which crosses every path;
The hidden boundary between
  God's patience and His wrath.

To cross that limit is to die,
  To die, as if by stealth.
It may not pale the beaming eye,
  Nor quench the glowing health.

The conscience may be still at ease,
  The spirits light and gay.
That which is pleasing still may please,
  And care be thrust away.

But on that forehead God hath set
  Indelibly a mark,
By man unseen, for man as yet
  Is blind and in the dark.

And still the doomed man's path below
  May bloom like Eden bloomed.
He did not, does not, will not know,
  Nor feel that he is doomed.

He feels, he sees, that all is well,
  His every fear is calmed.
He lives, he dies, he wakes in hell,
  Not only doomed, but damned.

Oh, where is that mysterious bourn,
  By which each path is crossed,
Beyond which God himself hath sworn
  That he who goes is lost?

> How long may men go on in sin,
> How long will God forbear?
> Where does hope end, and where begin
> The confines of despair?
>
> One answer from those skies is sent.
> "Ye who from God depart,
> While it is called to-day, repent,
> And harden not your heart."

> Therefore, as the Holy Spirit says, "Today, when
> you hear his voice, do not harden your hearts as in
> the rebellion, on the day of testing in the wilderness,
> where your fathers put me to the test and saw my
> works for forty years. Therefore I was provoked
> with that generation, and said, 'They always go astray
> in their hearts; they have not known my ways.' As I
> swore in my wrath, 'They shall never enter my rest.'"
> (Heb 3:7-11)

This quotation from Psalm 95:7-11 in the Greek
Bible forms the foundation for the second exhortation
in the Epistle to the Hebrews. Three Greek words with
similar sounds outline the three parts of the warning
and exhortation. In the best manuscripts they are:
apostasia (apostasy), *apistia* (unbelief or disbelief) and
apeitheia (disobedience).

When my book, *The Word of Truth*, used the word
apostasy, based on the Greek aorist infinitive *apostēnai*
(3:12) as the title for chapter 55, a great hue and cry
went up from the ignorant and dishonest, of which
Southern Baptists and many other conservative Calvinists have a thick mixture. Patience should prevail with
the ignorant, but the dishonest who know better require
more restraint. I am astonished that the very brief
article by Watson E. Mills in the *Mercer Dictionary of the*

Bible does not mention Hebrews 3:12. Mills rightly refers to Jeremiah 3:19, for the translation of the Hebrew *meshubah* with the Greek *apostasia* dominates the first seven chapters of Jeremiah. After the references to "perpetual backsliding" in Jeremiah 8:5 there are four shattering references to the apostasy which is unpardonable (9:16, 11:14, 15:1). This is precisely the teaching in Hebrews 6:4-6, 10:26, and 12:14. This Hebrews "treatise" (*logos*) seems almost certain to get the term *apostasia* from the prophet Jeremiah. Roy L. Honeycutt made a splendid summary of Jeremiah's view of apostasy in his book with the appropriate title, *Jeremiah: Witness Under Pressure* (Nashville: Convention Press, 1981, pp. 12-14).

Mill's article and the article in the same publication on Hebrews by Edgar V. McKnight ignore the possibility of apostasy in Hebrews. Gerald Borchert's *Warning and Assurance* (Broadman, 1987, pp. 156f.) calls Hebrews "a great book," and a "superb work" with a "marvelous message," but he tends to discount this teaching in the most "theological" document in the New Testament! H. H. Hobbs' influential manuscript, which was published for the Southern Baptist January Bible Study in 1954, argued that apostasy in English did not have the same meaning in the Greek *apostēnai*, translated "departing from the living God" in the Authorized Version. I have yet to find a Greek scholar who has been duly impressed. Neither before or after 1954 has a standard commentary agreed with Hobbs. I join William Tyndale, who in the 1534 edition of his first translation of the New Testament, even after a stout defense of many apostasy passages, asked: "And seinge the pistle agreeth to all the rest of the scripture, yet it be indifferently loked on, how shuldit not be ofautorye and taken for holye scrypture?" (Cambridge University Press, 1938, p. 502).

With an open mind and an open Bible let us now look at the three parts of the application of Psalm 95:7-11 to the danger and possibility of apostasy in Hebrews 3:12-4:11. The possibility and danger of *apostasia* (apostasy), from the aorist infinitive *apostēnai*, departing or falling away from the living God, dominates Hebrews 3:12-15. That is the possibility and the danger of apostasy when one turns away from the Living God to the worship of idols of men and false gods who are no gods at all. As Paul preached to the primitive Lycaonians at Lystra: they "should turn from these vain things to a living God who made the heaven and the earth and the sea and all that is in them" (Acts 14:15). Demetrius, a more cultured pagan in Ephesus of Asia, charged that Paul was ruining the sale of silver images of Artemis of Ephesus and that he was preaching "that gods made with hands are not gods" (Acts 19:26). In Athens, the cultural center of Greece, and in Rome, the political center where Hebrews was first read, this was a real danger, far more than theoretical speculation about the possibility of apostasy. What they needed was knowledge of the Unknown God whom they worshiped in ignorance (Acts 17:23, 30).

If Hebrews was written after Nero's burning of Rome in A.D. 64 and his suicide in A.D. 68 and before the fall of Jerusalem in A.D. 66-70, as I believe, this "word of exhortation" (Heb 13:22) was needed. After all, Peter had already been crucified and Paul beheaded. This was no time to speak smugly about "the eternal security of the believer." Hebrews has a theology of martyrdom.

They were told with an earnest plea "to exhort one another every day, as long as it is called 'today,' that none of you be hardened by the deceitfulness of sin" (3:13). Alas, superficial and sarcastic people, so-called friends, have told me that I did, indeed, take this verse seriously and literally, while they delight in "the deceitfulness of sin."

We are partakers (*metochoi*) of Christ "if only we hold our first confidence firm to the end" (3:14). *Metochoi* (partakers, sharers) is a favorite word for Joseph Barnabas (Heb 1:9; 3:1, 14; 6:4; 12:8).

This is a promise of security, but it is a conditional security, "if only we hold our confidence firm to the end" (3:14). The Greek word behind the translation "confidence" is *hupostasis*. A. T. Robertson says the word means "title-deed" when it is used in the only New Testament definition of faith (Heb 11:1). That meaning is also appropriate here, so we dare not teach that believers can lose their title-deed, even become atheists and unbelievers and live like reprobates, and still be eternally secure in their salvation, as some have done in their tirades against me. Seminary presidents, too, have felt the pressure of those trying to silence the presentation of true scriptural views. Some of us have warned for a decade that their interest is in the "takeover" of Southern Baptist agencies far more than the teaching of the Scriptures to which I have tried all my life to be faithful and to make them the final authority for all matters of faith and practice. Furthermore, I believe to use every trick in the trade to avoid the teachings of the Scriptures is a form of "the deceitfulness of sin" and of "hardness of the heart" (3:15).

'Today, when you hear his voice, do not harden
your hearts as in the rebellion.'

This warning began with a very high view of
Scripture: "So, as the Holy Spirit says":

'Today, when you hear his voice, do not harden
your hearts as in the rebellion, on the day of testing
in the wilderness ...'

A synonym for *apostasia* (apostasy) in 3:7-4:11 is
apistia (3:16-4:5), meaning "unbelief," lack of trust in
the promise of an inheritance in the Promised Land.
Those who came out of Egypt fell short of the Land
promised to Moses when they came out of Egypt. They
sinned and fell in the desert because of unbelief (3:19).
     Falling away (*apostēnai*) means the same as falling
short (*husterēkenai*, the perfect active infinitive of
hustereō, a word used as a present passive participle
also in Heb 11:37, "being destitute" and in 12:15, "falling short"). They did not reach the Promised Land
because of unbelief so the promise of a Sabbath in
Genesis 2:2 remains for the future.
     The falling away and the falling short prepares the
way for understanding the promise in the Davidic Psalm
95. These prepare the way for understanding the second synonym of *apostasia* (apostasy). This second synonym is *apeitheia* (disobedience; 4:6, 11). To the unfortunate chapter division in all translations is added the
mistranslation in the Authorized Version. The Greek
word for Joshua is the same as for Jesus, so the blunder
is understandable, but Hebrews 4 should read "Joshua,"
not Jesus. Psalm 95 is speaking of another day to be
fulfilled by Jesus in the future. Disobedience (*apeitheia*)

to him is far worse than disobedience to Moses and Joshua. "Let us, therefore, strive to enter that rest, that no one fall by the same example of disobedience" (4:11). Here it is unfortunate that the conclusion to the paragraph which should be 4:6-11 becomes the first verse of the next paragraph on the word of God in the Revised Standard Version. The New International Version is better here. The manuscript history to this important exhortation is confusing, but the Greek New Testament of the United Bible Societies seems best and is followed by the New International Version.

Repeat, hardness of heart is the result of *apostasia* (falling away), *apistia* (unbelief), and *apeitheia* (disobedience).

This hope for a Sabbath Rest for the People of God was not indeed realized in the time of Joshua (4:8), but the Promised Land did become a symbol of the Promised Sabbath Rest. A literal reading about an "inheritance" by the tribes of Israel in the Land of Canaan in Joshua 13-21 does not greatly stir the hopes of the faithful, even though the West Bank is greatly disputed today. But the symbolic use of the word "inheritance" for the Christian in the New Testament is one of our most inspirational themes.

I have never been asked to lead a Bible conference on Joshua 13-21, but my first favorite among Paul's Epistles was Ephesians. I rejoice that the last footnote in the 1990 translation of the New Revised Standard Version was suggested by me. It was at Ephesians 1:11, strangely omitted in the Revised Standard Version, although it does appear in Ephesians 1:14, 1:18 and 5:5.

It is true that the "inheritance" of a glorified land is found in Ezekiel, but Revelation alone in the New Testament quotes Ezekiel. The Sabbath Rest may also be behind the blessing in Revelation 14:13 which says: "Blessed are the dead who die in the Lord henceforth" and the response of the Spirit: "Blessed indeed that they may rest from their labors, for their deeds follow them." Am I the only one now that loves to sing with Samuel Stennett: "I am bound for the promised land"?

When a gifted Jewish artist confessed her faith in Jesus as the Messiah to me, with tears flowing down her impressive face, she said she believed that now she would make it to the Promised Land, with rests along the way in a sort of oasis journey through the desert. She began, as many early Christians did, in the mosaic of the Ravenna, Italy baptistry, praying Psalms 42 and 43, one Psalm in her Hebrew Bible. It is still one of my most helpful Psalms.

The Third Exhortation
Hebrews 5:11-6:20

This third exhortation of Hebrews became a pillar passage in the seventeenth century of modern Baptist history. This was especially seen in the place Hebrews 6:4-6 played in the formation of doctrine among the General Baptists. John Griffith, the gadfly among the Six Principle Baptists, summarized a century of discussion in a classic writing called *A Treatise Touching Falling from Grace*, 1707.

Until the publication of The Orthodox Creed in 1678, no General Baptists even attempted to come to terms with the Calvinistic confessions based upon the canons of the Synod of Dort in 1618 that condemned the disciples of James Arminius, then dead.

Particular Baptists rejected the teaching in Hebrews 2:9 which declared that Jesus, by the grace of God, "tasted death for every man." Great growth took place from the preaching of such leaders as Thomas Grantham, who edited his beliefs in his summary of doctrine called *Christianismus primitivus* ("Primitive Christianity"), also from 1678.

A second century saw the ministry of the so-called "Baptist Wesley," Dan Taylor, a Messenger in the movement called the New Connection of General Baptists. His doctrinal views were much the same as those of the great Thomas Grantham. We are blessed by his clear Confession of Faith, 1785. The stirring story of the great awakening among General Baptists is told in detail in *The History of the English General Baptists* by Adam Taylor (2 volumes, T. Bore, 1818).

After careful study of these and other General Baptists documents, I find them interpreting the New Testament very much the same way as I learned from the writings of A.T. Robertson, the greatest Southern Baptist Bible scholar when he died in 1934. It is astonishing to see many Southern Baptists still clinging to the creedalism of Calvinism. They fear Hebrews as much as the General Baptists loved it. It seems to me the time is overdue for serious study of the Scriptures and for a declaration of freedom from the bondage of Baptist Calvinism.

This third exhortation begins with a clear statement of the immature beliefs of those to whom the words were originally proclaimed. Hebrews 5:11-14 indicates that the immature believers had been Christians long enough to teach others, but they are still unable to digest solid food. "Solid food is for the mature, for those who have their faculties trained to distinguish good from evil" (5:14). Unless we are badly mistaken this is a condition that describes many, maybe the majority of church members today.

I have read most of the commentaries on Hebrews from John Calvin to the present, and the overwhelming conclusion is that these readers are viewed as believers, immature believers, to be sure, but they are believers. It seems that any person who can read even the English translation can see this. I challenge my reader to come to the text with an open Bible and an open mind. I have no doubt that the light will dawn on this sound and solid doctrine. Thinking is no sin.

Although I often find myself in agreement with

Alexander Campbell, I hereby find myself resisting his rationalism. Campbell died before the impact of the Wesleyan revival was assimilated and appreciated by the dominant Calvinism of his day.

As a young Texas preacher I read *He That Is Spiritual* by Lewis Sperry Chafer (Philadelphia: Sunday School Times, 1918). Chafer founded Dallas Theological Seminary. In my judgment Chafer was correct in his emphasis on the difference between the "carnal" and "spiritual" Christian in 1 Corinthians 3:1-3. The "carnal man" is an immature babe that is a believer in clear contrast with the "natural man" as an unbeliever (1 Cor 2:14). Here the translation of the Authorized (King James) Version is to be preferred to many modern translations and commentaries that confuse the "natural man" and the "carnal man." This leads to the error that there are just two types of man rather than the three with two types of Christians: the "carnal" and the "spiritual."

This same teaching seems clear in 1 Peter 2:1-3. This confusion seems to go back to the suppression of the Montanists who spoke of the Catholics as *psychici* (animal men) and of themselves as Spirit-filled pneumatics. The great Tertullian saw that the Montanists had the support of the Greek text and joined them! It was much as in our time when one is shunned and scorned as a "charismatic." The modern "carnal" Christian gets uncomfortable in compromise with the world.

Hebrews 6:1-3 has had an interesting history among General Baptists. Many of them became convinced that the six doctrines mentioned were fundamentals for faith and called themselves Six Principle Baptists. John Griffith stated his views in *God's Oracle and Christ's*

Doctrine or The Six Principles of the Christian Religion, 1655. Strangely enough Griffith did not emphasize that the six doctrines belong to the immature stage of the Christian Religion. Solid food is for the more mature Christians who can digest the solid food taught in Hebrews.

I belong to a Baptist church where the pastor practices the laying on of hands after immersion, the so-called Fourth Principle of John Griffith and the Six Principle Baptists. I have practiced it myself, but I think it belongs only to the elementary stage of the Christian life. It should be used, if used at all, as a part of initiation into the Church, not graduation. It signifies new born babes, not full grown fellowship. I most certainly do not believe the theory that only by the laying on of hands does one receive the Holy Spirit.

That is why most General Baptists were unwilling to accept the arguments of John Griffith and the Six Principle Baptists. That is as wrong as the argument that only in baptism is the Spirit received. I believe in both "the teachings of Baptism and the laying on of hands," and all the other six principles, but I believe we need to go on to maturity, even if we neglect some of these. They belong to the *bene esse* (well being) of the church, but not to the *esse* (essential nature without which there is no salvation). Alexander Campbell was right when he saw only "the faith and intelligence" of the believer as the one essential (*Christian Baptism,* p. 219). Yet in 1826 another famous Campbell, John McLeod Campbell, was tried for heresy by the Presbyterian Calvinists in Scotland for believing in the "assurance of faith" and that Jesus, in his death, "tasted death for every man" (Heb 2:9).

Much harm and hindrance has also been done by making such things as circumcision, baptism, laying on of hands, speaking in tongues, and others to be absolute essentials for faith and forgiveness, regeneration and baptism in the Spirit — yet I accept them all!

It is only within recent times that questions have been raised about "the resurrection of the dead, and of eternal judgment" (Heb 6:2). Of course, there was a form of Gnosticism in the early church which preached a "gangrene" Gospel. Hymenaeus and Philetus, two Gnostic teachers, "wandered away from the truth" saying that "the resurrection has already taken place, and they destroyed the faith of some" (2 Tim 2:17f, cf. 1 Tim 1:19). Much of the preaching in the Calvinist tradition has ignored or denied that there are those who have "shipwrecked their faith" (1 Tim 1:20), but those who have been influenced by Arminianism have not hesitated to point out the graveyards of wrecked ships.

It seems that the time has come to go to the root of this Gnostic heresy which seems to surface more and more in our time. When I preach Paul's view of immortality as a gift from God and reject the view of the natural or essential immortality of the soul in Plato and Aristotle, I often find people upset by the teachings of Paul in 1 Corinthians 15:35-58, his classic passage, which continues to echo to the very end of the Pauline Epistles (2 Cor 5:1-5; Rom 1:23; 2:7; 1 Tim 6:16, 2 Tim 1:10). The bodily resurrection at the *Parousia* (Second Coming) seems to put even some of the most conservative people in a state of shock. They seem unable to believe that the majority of Christian theologians, both Catholic and Protestant, have been preaching and teaching Plato, Aristotle, and Kant.

My friend Oscar Cullmann found this out when he gave the Ingersol Lectures at Harvard University, no conservative Bible College by far. The very title of his

lectures awoke many from dogmatic slumber: *Immortality
of the Soul or Resurrection from the Dead?* (1958) His
lectures along with several responses is an example of
the type of debate needed more and more in our time
(Krister Stendahl, ed., *Immortality*, Macmillan, 1965). For
years this was required reading for my students, but
Plato and Aristotle still ruled much of Christendom.
Many Liberal Protestants shift to the moral arguments
of Immanuel Kant. Paul's view of immortality was
even condemned as heresy by the Fifth Lateran Council,
1513. Even the *New Oxford Dictionary* of the Christian
Church says that Paul's view of immortality "has nowa-
days but few defenders among serious Christian theologians." They think immortality is based on the nature
of man rather than the nature of God.

The phrase "eternal judgment" introduced a rising
debate anew, especially by Edward Fudge in his challenging book that will be mentioned again when Hebrews 12:29 is discussed (*The Fire that Consumes*,
Providential Press, 1982). Fudge challenges the as-
sumption that "eternal" always means "everlasting."
The eternal judgment does not seem to mean that judgment goes on and on forever. It seems to mean the
judgment that is final and will never be repeated. (See
Fudge, pp. 44-48, on other passages in Hebrews that use
"words of actions" with *aiōnios*, e.g. 5:9; 9:12. Cf. also
on "eternal sin" in Mark 3:29 and "eternal punishment"
in Matt 25:46, and especially "eternal destruction" in 2
Thess 1:9). "Eternal judgment" is action never to be
repeated. This has stirred up a very fruitful debate
which I eagerly join.

"Eternal punishment" then in Matthew 25:46 does
not mean "eternal punishing," punishing that goes on
and on forever, but a punishment that is final and never

to be repeated. The word *kolasis,* from *kolazō,* to "lop off," is usually translated "punishment" and means to be lopped off, and that lopping off does not go on and on forever as the "Rotisserie" view of retribution insists. This agrees with Paul's view that after the final judgment God will be "all in all" and with the passages in Paul that speak of the "destruction" of the wicked and the passages in John that say the wicked "perish." It brings us back to the first Psalm which most know from memory! I must urge the thoughtful reader to study very carefully and prayerfully the very full discussion of this topic by Fudge. I need help if he is not correct, for I have wavered on this conclusion since I, at the ripe age of seventeen, preached my third sermon on Psalm 1 in the Baptist Church in Farmers Branch, Texas. I do not believe Fudge's exposition of Scripture and Christian theologians has many, if any, errors.

Hebrews 6:4-6 reinforces the belief that this exhortation is for believers, not unbelievers. The five aorist participles make it clear that those in verse 6 who are in danger of falling away are the same as those described in 6:4 and following. Endless efforts have tried to explain this away so that conservative Calvinism can be preserved.

It is not necessary to go beyond Hebrews to see that those who have been once for all time enlightened are believers. In Hebrews 10:32 it is said that those who endured a great conflict of suffering for their faith had already passed out of darkness into light. At least the *First Apology* (Chap 61) of Justin the Martyr in the second century said that initiation into the Church by baptism was known as *phōtismos,* enlightenment.

"Tasting of the heavenly gift" describes becoming a believer as "tasting to see that the Lord is gracious," a picture borrowed from Psalm 34:8 ("O taste and see that the Lord is good"). This is a description of those who like "newborn babes, long for the pure spiritual milk that you may grow up to salvation" in 1 Peter 2:3. There is no reason to believe it has a different meaning in Hebrews 6:5.

The "mere taster" theory goes back at least to Calvin in 1549 (*Commentaries*, p. 76; also *Institutes* III. ii.11), but numerous sermons and Sunday School lessons have blundered with expositors like John Owen and John Brown. The major source of the "mere taster" theory in England seems to be the eight volumes by Owen (1668-84). Brown's 1862 *Commentary* has been chosen to represent the modern Geneva Commentaries, published by the Banner of Truth Trust. Brown falsely says: "Tasting does not include eating, much less digesting and turning into nourishment what is so tasted" (p. 285).

Such a theory would lead to calling Jesus a "mere taster" when he "tasted death for every man" (Heb 2:9). Of course, rigid Calvinism, with the theory of limited atonement, has consistently denied that "Jesus tasted death for every man." They are unable to refute the General Baptists who use Hebrews 2:9 as a favorite text. They simply ban them with a majority vote. As the Apostle Paul said of his opponents in Corinth: "Not that we venture to class or compare ourselves with some of those who commend themselves. But when they measure themselves by one another, and compare themselves with one another, they are without understanding" (2 Cor 10:12).

Partaking of the Holy Spirit is another way of saying they are partakers of Christ (Heb 3:14). The same word (*metoxous*) is used to describe those who share their lives together, "comrades" (1:9). These "comrades" (*metoxous*) are the same as the "partakers" (*metochoi*) of the heavenly calling (3:1) and the "partakers (*metochoi*) of Christ" (3:14). The term is used a fifth time in Hebrews when it is the sons of God who are described as those who are "partakers" (*metochoi*) of discipline or chastisement (12:8). They are "true sons" not "illegitimate children" (NIV), (*nothoi*, "bastards" in the Authorized King James Version).

If this is not sufficient proof that those in danger of apostasy or falling away are at least immature believers, the word "tasted" is used again; this time they have "tasted the good Word of God, and the "powers of the world to come" or "a coming age."

I know of no other passage in the New Testament that is clearer about the beginning of the Christian life, yet John Brown says they "seem to intimate that the possession of these by unrenewed men was not very uncommon in that age; at any rate, they plainly show that their possession and an unregenerate state were by no means incompatible" (p. 286). He is like a woodpecker pounding at Stone Mountain.

No wonder Charles Spurgeon said he was "a very bad Calvinist"! He was not a Calvinist at all when he prayed: "Lord, hasten to bring in all Thine elect, and then elect some more." Spurgeon confronted what Paul would call a "super apostle" (2 Cor 11:5; 12:11) or a "false apostle" (2 Cor 11:13) in James Wells of the Gospel Standard Church at the Surrey Tabernacle. Wells was sarcastically mentioned by Spurgeon as "King James" when Wells said he doubted that Spurgeon was saved and knew he was a liberal for having D.L. Moody in his pulpit. The warm friendship between Charles Spurgeon and D.L. Moody should be more publicized.

Southern Baptist Seminary has a painting of Spurgeon given to us by the Moody Bible Institute! A good picture of this famous conflict with Wells is found in A.C. Underwood, *A History of English Baptists* (London, 1947, pp. 203-8. (Information of this came in a letter from Ronald F. Deering, January 12, 1990.)

After all this it is possible to commit apostasy, as the Revised Standard Version translates the aorist participle *parapesontas*, which means literally "having fallen by the wayside," from *para*, "alongside," and *piptō*, "fall." Webster's says apostasy means the "renunciation of a religious faith" or "abandonment of a previous loyalty." Those who argue that apostasy does not have the same meaning in Greek as it does in English are doing special pleading. A.T. Robertson says the Greek text "bluntly denies the possibility of renewal for apostates from Christ (cf. Heb 3:2; 4:2). It is a terrible picture and cannot be toned down" (*Word Pictures in the New Testament*, V. 375). H. H. Hobbs tries to refute Robertson by saying that the writer does, indeed, assume that those described had been "regenerated" in "genuine spiritual experience" but that apostasy means they are only in "the peril of an arrested Christian growth by which these Hebrew Christians are in peril of falling short of their ultimate destiny in Christian behavior and service" (*Studies in Hebrews*, Convention Press, 1954, pp. 52-57). While this view may be more acceptible to most Baptists, I still think he is doing expedient special pleading. If my reader thinks I am not a good Baptist, let him read *A Treatise Touching Falling from Grace* by John Griffith (1707) the great General Baptist Messenger. As already said, it was not until The Orthodox Creed of 1678 that the General Baptists, under pressure, even tipped their hats to the Calvinistic conservatism that opposed both evangelism and missions. It would make little sense to speak of the impossibility of renewal again (*palin*) of apostates if they had never been renewed in the first place, as John Brown so blindly argues. Such apostates do, indeed, "crucify the son of God on their own account and hold him up to contempt" (6:6), and those who deceive people about such danger only increase the crowd at the crucifixion.

How can one improve on the illustration used by the author in 6:7 and following? The plot of land that responds to tilling and rain in a positive way and "brings forth vegetation" "receives a blessing from God" (6:7). On the other hand, "if it bears thorns and thistles, it is worthless and near to being cursed; its end is to be burned" (6:8).

The word "worthless" is the same as the one translated "castaway" in the King James Version of 1 Corinthians 9:27 (*adokimos*), which is also translated "reprobates" in the plural in 2 Corinthians 13:5. That meaning is in perfect harmony with the word "cursed" (*kataras*) in the near future and burned in the end, the final outcome, *telos*.

The teaching here is the same as the parable of the sower as interpreted in Luke 8:13 and following. The superficial professors "believe for a while and in a time of temptation fall away" (8:13). These are the "down and out" disciples. Those who fell among thorns are the "up and outs," those who "fell among thorns" after they heard and then let "the cares and riches and pleasures of this life" so dominate them that "their fruit does not mature" (8:14). What a picture of the modern "yuppies."

Borchert argues that apostasy in Hebrews 6:6 is not used as it is in Hebrews 3:12 where the Greek word is *apostēnai*, meaning "falling away" (p. 199, n. 36). It is true that the aorist participle *parapesontas* is used in 6:6 and the aorist infinitive *apostēnai* in 3:12, but the words mean much the same. What is the difference in experience between "falling away" in 3:12 and "having fallen alongside" in 6:6? None! The Revised Standard Version is not in error. At least Borchert does see that John Brown's 1862 argument (seen also in the *Criswell Study Bible*) of lurching out to grasp at Hebrews 6:9 is "a smoke screen," in vivid contrast with another honorable Scot named I. Howard Marshall at Aberdeen (p. 199, n. 35). Of course, the preacher hoped his exhortations would deter people from apostasy. Otherwise, why exhort them? If there was no danger, why any warning at all? Salvation in Hebrews 6:9-12 is described as love (6:10), hope (6:11), and faith (6:12), the "better things that belong to salvation" (6:9).

Love is seen in serving the saints. If Barnabas is the author of Hebrews, as Tertullian thought in the third century and as I have long believed, then it is clear why the money this "Son of encouragement" put at the apostles' feet from the sale of a field for distribution to the poor saints of Jerusalem was looked upon as a powerful example in contrast with the lying hypocrisy of Ananias and Sapphira (Acts 4:36-5:6).

Hope is the shorthand for the things hoped for and summarized in the great chapter on hope in the fifth and final exhortation in chapter 12. After chapter 11 on faith and chapter 12 on hope the author returns to the theme of love as that which should continue (13:1) before more practical applications are added as an appendix.

Faith is the *hypostasis*, the assurance or very title deed of things "hoped" for, the conviction or *elengchos*

"of things not seen" (Heb 11). There is no other scripture equal to this definition of faith. The word *pistei* (by
faith) is used seven times to summarize the history of
faith through Sarah (11:12). After the first summary
(11:13-16) the word *pistei* is used eleven more times
(11:17-31) through another great woman of the faith,
surprisingly, Rahab the harlot. Matthew 1:5 gives us
another shock by including her as the first great woman
in the genealogy of Jesus before the Virgin Mary (1:23).
The second summary in Hebrews 11 takes us from the
judges to the freedom fighter Judas Maccabaeus (Judas
the Hammerer) who drove out the Syrians in 165 B.C.

It is well known that Hebrews 11:35-40 uses 2
Maccabees 7:9, 14; 5:27; 6:12-7:42; 6:11, and 10:6. That is
one of the reasons the Christians of the fourth century
shifted the celebration of Christmas from May 20 to
December 25 when the Jews already celebrated Hanuk-
kah, the Dedication of the Temple after its desecration.
Perhaps the practical reason for the shift for both Jews
and Christians was to avoid conflict with both the Jewish Passover and the Christian Holy Week.

Both Jews and Christians thus become freedom
fighters against the idolatry and the immorality of the
pagan Roman Saturnalia. How stupid it is for Christmas to be celebrated with more lust and liquor than
usual and call ourselves Christians.

Abraham is the model by which those who persevere inherit the promise (6:13-20). Abraham, "having
patiently endured, obtained the promise" (6:15). Had
he not "patiently endured" he would not have "obtained the promise." How can one, in the light of this
model, argue that without perseverance we have "eternal security" and will obtain the promise?

With perseverance the promise will be inherited.

"We have this as a sure and steadfast anchor of the soul, a hope that enters into the shrine behind the curtain, where Jesus has gone as a forerunner on our behalf, having become a high priest forever after the order of Melchizedek" (6:19f.). In the language of sailors on a ship the forerunner (*prodromos*) is the sailor who takes the anchor to shore so that those who remain on the ship may land safely. Jesus is the *prodromos*. We need only to remain aboard to be saved from the storm. In the language of Acts 28:31 and in the words of Paul: "Unless these men stay in the ship, you cannot be saved."

It is unfortunate that the New Testament teaching on "the perseverance of the saints" has been displaced by the idea of a false "security of the believer." The believer is secure as long as he perseveres, but this understanding of perseverance (*hypomonē*) has been repudiated by those who glibly speak of "the security of believers" who have become unbelievers and atheists and live like pagans, as W.O. Vaught has argued in his book called *Believe Plus Nothing* (1983, p. 28).

On May 3, 1873, J. R. Graves, one of the founders of Southern Baptist Landmarkism, rejected the term "the perseverance of the saints" and proposed the term "the security of believers" to replace it. He thought the term "perseverance" suggested human endurance as a condition for security, as is the case. This was adopted by his disciples as a dogma and by the beginning of the twentieth century "the security of believers" had become known as "eternal security," as in the widely circulated sermon by J. M. Carroll at Ashland Avenue Baptist Church, Lexington, Kentucky, called "The Eternal Security of the Blood-Bought Believers" (see more details in my book, *The Word of Truth*, pp. 362f.). The outcome was the dangerous doctrine expounded by W.O. Vaught in a tape (Oct 24, 1982), attacking me, more radical than his book printed later.

The perseverance of the saints in Hebrews 6:13-20 calls for the "patient endurance" demonstrated when Abraham obeyed God's command to offer up his son Isaac. By Abraham keeping the conditions God kept the promise to bless him, as in Genesis 22:16-17.

The path to the promise of God in Christ is that type of patient endurance supported by God's oath to bless those who trust and obey (Heb 6:17-20). God will not lie. That is one of the impossible things mentioned in Hebrews 6:4, 6:18, and 11:6, but perseverance is the path and condition to the fulfillment of God's promise. Salvation is conditional, by grace "through faith (*dia pisteōs*)," but there is no grace for those who have no faith. And without faith it is impossible to please him. For "whoever would draw near to God must believe that he is and that he rewards those who seek him" (11:6).

This is a far cry from the Calvinism that declares that God unconditionally gives faith to the elect few but leaves the non-elect without either grace or faith. Double predestination is a dangerous doctrine. That was the problem with which such saints as Andrew Fuller and Charles Spurgeon wrestled. Thanks to God they were very bad Calvinists and very good Christians! Spurgeon's sermon, "Compell Them to Come In," for which he was accused of Arminianism, has the message that made him and his friend D.L. Moody the greatest pastor and the greatest evangelist of the nineteenth century. Let us join with Spurgeon in his oft quoted prayer: "Lord, hasten to bring in Thine elect, then elect some more."

The Fourth Exhortation
Hebrews 10:19-39

Of the five exhortations about the possibility of apostasy in Hebrews, the fourth is perhaps most neglected and rejected, yet it is the least ambiguous in meaning.

The fourth exhortation has three paragraphs. The first may be called: The New and Living Way — Hebrews 10:19-25. If, as I believe, Hebrews was written to Christian believers under persecution, either in Rome or Jerusalem, the siege of Jerusalem between A. D. 66-70 offers the best background of understanding. The crucial question is whether the destruction of the Temple would mark the departure of God's presence from Jerusalem.

The belief stated here is that the death of Jesus was the "once-for- all" sacrifice that made unnecessary the repetition of the Day of Atonement, the holiest day in the year in Judaism. Jesus has become "the new and living way" into the sanctuary in which he is both high priest and sacrifice "over the house of God." The earthly sanctuary may pass away, but the heavenly sanctuary now fully revealed in Jesus will never pass away.

The fourth exhortation introduced with faith, hope and love is really a preview to the last three chapters of Hebrews with the greatest chapter on faith in the Bible (11), one of the most important chapters on hope (12), and concluding admonitions introduced with a call to brotherly love (13).

Each of the so called theological virtues is introduced with "let us." Once, when I was being interpreted in another language, the congregation was told that I was about to speak on "rabbit food" ("lettuce"). Not exactly, but it is definitely "soul food" for the faithful.

We are to "draw near with a true heart in full assurance of faith, with our hearts sprinkled clean from an evil conscience and our bodies washed with pure water" (10:22). Some of the most important words for faithfulness appear. The "true heart" expresses the positive side of genuine trust in a Hebrew way, while "evil conscience" is the negative side described in a Greek way. Heart and conscience are at other places key words in Hebrews.

A most instructive term is "full assurance" (*plērophoria*), a much stronger term than assurance. With "full assurance" believers become less likely to go back into unbelief. It is the lack of "full assurance" that is so dangerous. To deny this danger for ourselves and others is deceptive talk.

The second call is to "hold fast the confession of our hope without wavering, for he who promised is faithful." The faithfulness of God is ever true, but it is our unfaithfulness that may be in danger. A faithful saying says (2 Tim 2:11-13):

> If we have died with him,
>   we shall also live with him;
> if we endure with him,
>   we shall also reign with him;
> if we deny him,
>   he will also deny us;
> if we are faithless,
>   he remains faithful—
> for he cannot deny himself.

Those who use this saying to support the belief that a believer can later become an unbeliever and an atheist and still be eternally secure in his salvation lead people astray. (See W. O. Vaught, *Believe Plus Nothing,* 1983, p. 28 for such teaching.) The third call is to "consider how to stir up one another to love and good works." These words are written in the week of my father's death; he died January 7, 1985. I have written and spoken millions and millions of words to stir up people to love, but my Dad had a fifth grade education and was a man of few words. I am left with the question if his life of love and good works, mentioned in so many ways, was not more acceptable to God. Time after time I remember the cold mornings on a small farm and ranch when he would rise early to stir up the coals and put on more wood for the comfort of his family.

One morning I saw these words in the *Dallas Morning News* that was thrown regularly on our porch.

> I like my friends like I like my fires,
> Open and ruddy to the seasoned core,
> Sweet fibered and hickory hearted,
> The sort you can warm your life by.

The two old fireplaces at each end of the old two-storied house picture the prayer that was created in my heart among the simple pioneer people at home and in little one-room churches in those days. I have long believed the most important thing done by the church is "meeting" or as Hebrews 10:25 says: "Not neglecting to meet together, as is the habit of some, but encouraging one another, and all the more as you see the day drawing near." We may try to do things through the churches in a bigger way, but we will never be "church" in a better way.

Apostasy as Willful Sin (Hebrews 10:26-31)

I trust that the reader has already read chapter 55 of my book *The Word of Truth* in which I discuss this biblical doctrine in a larger context. In the introduction to that chapter I explained that I was using the word apostasy as it was used in Hebrews 3:12, where the Greek for "departing" or "falling away" is *apostēnai*. I have already pointed out the complete omission of this word in the article by Watson E. Mills on apostasy in the *Mercer Dictionary of the Bible*.

I also explained how Hebrews is the major New Testament writing on apostasy, although I quote from 26 of the 27 New Testament books in support of the view expressed in the five long warnings against the danger of apostasy (2:1-4; 3:7-4:13; 6:4-6; 10:26-31 and 12:14-17).

I have chosen to expand part of the fourth warning, which is Hebrews 10:26-31. Remember that I believe the supreme authority for all faith and practice is the Scripture. It is to be put above all human tradition whether they be creeds, confessions or popular clichés. I am completely committed to Article I of the *Abstract of Principles* of The Southern Baptist Theological Seminary where I have been a teacher for 37 years. Article I says: "The Scriptures of the Old and New Testament were given by inspiration of God, and are the only sufficient, certain and authoritative rules of all saving knowledge, faith and obedience." At the beginning of Article XVIII the *Abstract of Principles* says: "God alone is Lord of the conscience; and He hath left it free from the doctrines and commandments of men which are in anything contrary to His Word, or not contained in it." To these principles of Scripture and conscience I am completely committed.

There are three points in Hebrews 10:26.

1. If We Go on Sinning Deliberately.
What is willful or deliberate sin? What does the
literal translation of the first line in Hebrews 10:26
mean when it says: "If we keep on sinning deliberately
or willfully"?
The Old Testament background to this passage is
Numbers 15:30. If you begin reading at Numbers 15:22
you will note that sins done out of human weakness
and ignorance can be forgiven. These are called errors
and sins committed unwittingly. The worst of human
sins, even adultery and murder, can be forgiven.
There is only one sin for which there is no sacrifice
and no forgiveness. That is called presumptuous sin or
sin committed with a high hand (Num 15:30).
The best recent statement on the meaning of willful sin by a Baptist writer is in a book called *Hebrews*
(Tyndale, 1976), dedicated to W. A. Criswell and written by a past President of the Southern Baptist Convention, James T. Draper, Jr. His excellent summary says:

> Here is someone who has been saved and yet
> maliciously, willfully, deliberately plots to disobey
> God, to rebel against God. This does not refer to an
> accidental sin. It is not merely an isolated act of sin
> or lust or passion. This text refers to careful, pre-
> meditated, deliberate sin against God by a believer.
> It shows a Christian who acts knowing that his deed
> is against God, against his will, against his purpose.
> And in spite of it all, he shakes his fist in the face of
> God and says, "Leave me alone. I will do as I please."
> It is willful premeditated rebellion (pp. 278f.).

Excellent statement! Excellent statement!

2. After Receiving the Knowledge of the Truth.

In the interest of brevity I will again make reference to the excellent statement on the meaning of knowledge (*epignōsis*) in the book, *Hebrews*, by James T. Draper, Jr. Herschel H. Hobbs argued the same in his *Studies in Hebrews* (Convention Press, 1954) and his *Hebrews* (Broadman Press, 1971), first published as *How to Follow Jesus*. I am very happy to agree with these two outstanding pastors on these first two points.

James T. Draper, Jr. must have used a Greek lexicon or a good concordance when he listed 2 Peter 1:2, 1 Timothy 2:4, 2 Timothy 3:7, Ephesians 1:17, 18; 4:13, and Romans 10:2 to demonstrate the point that *epignōsis* (knowledge) really means "full knowledge," as H. H. Hobbs argued many years earlier.

Strangely enough James T. Draper, Jr. did not use the most powerful passage on *epignōsis* (full knowledge). That passage is 2 Peter 2:20-22. The noun is used once in 2:20 and the verb is used twice in 2:21.

Now read carefully and prayerfully 2 Peter 2:20 in the Revised Standard version. Let me put two questions. First, how can they get "tangled again in them and overcome" if they were not first tangled, then got untangled, then "tangled again in them and overcome"? Second, how can the "last state" be worse than the "first state" in which they were entangled in "the defilements of the world" and a "last state" when they went back to the "defilements of the world"? It is clear that they went back to the state before believing.

Now look at 2 Peter 2:21 where the verb for knowledge (*epignōskō*) is used twice. Another question! Would it not be necessary to go some distance on "the way of righteousness" before they could turn back from the holy commandments delivered to them? You cannot turn back before you have gone forward.

This great passage on the apostasy of those who have full knowledge of the truth is sealed with Proverbs 26:11 in 1 Peter 2:22.

3. There No Longer Remains a Sacrifice for Sins.

Those who accept the first two points made by Hobbs and Draper run into great difficulty in their defense of tradition over Scripture when they come to this third point in Hebrews 10:26. Some argue that the sacrifice of Christ was for sin, not for sins (see especially H. H. Hobbs), but this will not hold. This is the tenth time in ten chapters that Hebrews has made reference to sins. In Hebrews 10:12, just above Hebrews 10:26, are these words: "But when Christ had offered for all time a single sacrifice for sins, he sat down on the right hand of God" (RSV). Do as Draper did on full knowledge (*epignōsis*) and look up all the references to sin and sins in Hebrews and you will discover that any distinction between Christ's sacrifice for sins and for sin is without foundation in fact.

Still others try to get out of the corner into which they have painted themselves by appealing to the word "judgment" (*krisis*). Judgment (*krisis*) in Hebrews 10:27 has the same meaning as judgment in Hebrews 9:27 and following, which says:

> And just as it is appointed to men to die once and after that comes judgment (*krisis*), so Christ having been offered once to bear the sins of many, will appear a second time not to deal with sin but to save those who are eagerly waiting for him.

If I had the opportunity to preach a second sermon it would surely be on Hebrews 9:23-29, but I am not given that much time.   Hebrews 10:27 is not speaking of the judgment seat of Christ where rewards are received or withheld from the saved.   Had he had in mind the judgment seat of Christ, he would have used the Greek word *bema* (cf. 2 Cor 5:10).

There is only a third phrase that is often neglected by many, but it is the clincher for what follows.   The phrase "fury of fire that will consume the adversaries" comes from Isaiah 26:11 where Isaiah 26:10 calls the "adversaries" or the "enemies" of God "the wicked." Then Isaiah 26:14 described them as those who will have no part in the resurrection to life.   There is no question that Hebrews 10:27 describes the destiny of the damned.   The reason for this destiny of the damned is described in great detail by the contrast between the punishment (*timoria*) of sinners in the Old Covenant of the Old Testament and punishment (*timoria*) of apostate sinners in the New Covenant of the New Testament.

Hebrews 10:28 quotes Deuteronomy 32:35-36 as follows: "A man who has violated the law of Moses dies without mercy at the testimony of two or three witnesses."   Those who have no sacrifice for their sins and are therefore damned have three witnesses against them.

First, they have stomped the Son of God under their feet (10:29). Do you really believe a person can stomp the Son of God under his feet and still be saved? Do you?

Second, the apostates have treated as unholy the blood of the new covenant with which they were sanctified.   The use of the singular in Hebrews 10:29 brings the sin to each one of us.   Do you really believe that a person can treat the blood of Christ as profane or unholy and still be saved?   Do you?

Under the old covenant, as Hebrews 9:22 says,

almost everything is purified with blood, and without the shedding of blood there is no forgiveness of sins. The blood of Christ is the basis for the forgiveness of all sins of all times. No person has ever been saved and no person will ever be saved who has profaned the blood of Christ.

The third witness against apostates says they have "outraged the Spirit of grace" (10:29). The nearest thing to this in the Old Testament is the grieving of God's Holy Spirit in Isaiah 63:10 which says:

> But they rebelled
> and grieved his Holy Spirit;
> therefore he turned to be their enemy,
> and himself fought against them.

This is quoted in part in Ephesians 4:30.

Let me ask again. Do you really believe that a person can come before God at the final judgment with no sacrifice for his sins and still be saved? Do you really believe one can stomp the Son of God under his feet, treat as unholy the blood of Christ of the New Covenant with which he was sanctified, and outrage "the Spirit of grace" and come before God at the final judgment as a "saved" person? Do you?

The answer to all these questions is found in the conclusion of Hebrews 10:30 and following: "For we know him who said, 'Vengeance is mine, I will repay.'"

The Perseverance of the Saints

Preaching on the previous paragraph (10:26-31) precipitated a crisis in my teaching career of forty years, so it has been pondered carefully for any evidence of error. None has been found and not one person has made an effort to refute my exegesis. This following paragraph (10:32-39) has only strengthened my sense of exegetical integrity.

The behavior here described is definitely that of believers who are under pressure to become unbelievers again. The "after receiving the knowledge of the truth" (10:26) is now "after you were enlightened" (10:32). The old cliché that says they had illumination without salvation is as impossible here as in the previous reference (6:4). Illumination "belongs to salvation" (6:9). (See also the exposition of 6:4-6.)

The perseverance of the saints (10:32-34) is introduced with a vivid picture of the persecution of the saints. It is possible that a passage in the *Annals* of Tacitus (15:44) has reference to the same ordeal of suffering and loss of property. After Nero burned Rome, July 19, A.D. 64, he looked for a scapegoat among the Christians:

> Accordingly, an arrest was made of all who pleaded guilty; then, upon their information, an immense multitude was convicted, not so much of the crime of firing the city, as of hatred against mankind. Mockery of every sort was added to their deaths. Covered with the skins of beasts, they were torn by dogs and perished, or were nailed to crosses, or were doomed to the flames and burnt, to serve as nightly illumination, when daylight had expired. (*The Complete Works of Tacitus*, The Modern Library, 1942, p. 381.)

Tacitus clearly did not think the Christians were guilty and speaks only of the "glut of one man's cruelty."

The Roman destiny of Hebrews has been challenged since the studies of Qumran have accumulated.

Moses Stuart, as far back as 1828, argued for a Palestinian origin and destiny of the letter. (See George Wesley Buchanan, *To the Hebrews*, The Anchor Bible, vol. 36, New York, Doubleday and Co., 1981, pp. 255-267.) A Palestinian Christian (Barnabas?, cf. Acts 4:36) may have written from Caesarea to former Essenes now Christians in Jerusalem during the Jewish War of A. D. 66-73, described in such detail in Josephus' Jewish War. In any case the contents indicate a crisis in the community in which many were tempted to escape from suffering by apostasy (2:1-4, 3:7-4:11; 6:1-29; 10:19-39; 12:1-29). The appeal to Habakkuk 2:3-4 as the call for perseverance (10:35-39) does suggest an Essene background. A commentary on Habakkuk was found at Qumran. By the translation of *hypomonē* as "perseverance" in the New International Version (10:36, 12:1) a distorted term has been given a more biblical meaning by putting the emphasis on the future continuation of the Christian life rather than the mere commencement in the past. That is why salvation always has a future reference in Hebrews (1:14; 2:10; 5:9; 6:9; 9:28).

The Fifth Exhortation
Hebrews 12:1-29

The fifth and last exhortation in Hebrews constitutes one of the most important and balanced chapters in the New Testament. For the third time a sin is mentioned for which there is no remedy (12:15-17) as God is described as both Father (12:1-17) and Judge (12:18-29).

God as Father
Using both the frame of a Greek stadium (12:1-17) and the Hebrew Sinai (12:18-29), the great cloud of witnesses of chapter 11 who have departed this life are described as spectators in an amphitheatre with those that follow after down below in the arena. Those in the arena are called upon to lay aside the weights on their feet and their robes of sin that cling so easily that they may better run the race before them. The weights on their feet represent the many occasional sins for which there is forgiveness when confessed, but the besetting sin is the sin of apostasy from Christ. This is all in agreement with the distinction between forgivable sins of ignorance and weakness and the high-handed sin for which there is no forgiveness in Numbers 15:27-31.

The translation of *hupomonē* as "perserverence," rescues a good word whose original meaning has been greatly diluted by the notion that all in the race, regardless of their belief and behavior, are sure winners. Those who persevere to the end are the "real believers" about which the New Hampshire Confession of Faith of 1833 spoke when it said in Article XI, "of the Perseverance of Saints":

> "[we believe] that such only are real believers as endure to the end; that their persevering attachment to Christ is the grand mark which distinguishes them from mere professors."

It is interesting to note how the word "mere" was revised to "superficial" in 1853. This was the basis for the much weaker article in The Baptist Faith and Message of 1963 which simply says: "All true believers endure to the end." Nothing is said about those who do not endure (Mark 13:13). Could they not just quote Hebrews 6:4-6? Nothing is said about apostasy as it is found in the New Testament, especially Hebrews. Paul was not as sure about others and himself in 1 Corinthians 8:11, 9:24-27, and 10:6-13, as many smugly assert.

In Hebrews 12:1 and following we are exhorted:

> Therefore, since we are surrounded by so great a cloud of witnesses, let us also lay aside every weight, and sin which clings so closely, and let us run with perseverance the race that is set before us, looking to Jesus the pioneer and perfecter of our faith, who for the joy that was set before him endured the cross, despising the shame, and is seated at the right hand of the throne of God.
>
> Consider him who endured from sinners such hostility against himself, so that you may not grow weary or fainthearted. In your struggle against sin you have not yet resisted to the point of shedding your blood. And have you forgotten the exhortation which addresses you as sons?—

"My son, do not regard lightly the discipline of the Lord, nor lose courage when you are punished by him. For the Lord disciplines him whom he loves, and chastises every son whom he receives."
It is for discipline that you have to endure. God is treating you as sons; for what son is there whom his father does not discipline? If you are left without discipline in which all have participated, then you are illegitimate children and no sons. Besides this, we have had earthly fathers to discipline us and we respected them. Shall we not much more be subject to the Father of spirits and live? For they discipline us for a short time at their pleasure, but he disciplines us for our good, that we may share his holiness. For the moment all discipline seems painful rather than pleasant; later it yields the peaceful fruit of righteousness to those who have been trained by it.

Those who persevere are called upon to consider the example of Jesus and to expect discipline from the Lord when they go astray (12:3-11).

Paul thought that one may lose his reward, his health, his life and even his salvation (1 Cor 3:15; 5:5; 11:31; 8:11; 9:27; 10:12). The first three of these passages are constantly used, while the last three are neglected, to deny the possibility of the loss of salvation by James T. Draper, (*Hebrews*, Tyndale, 1976, pp. 278ff), who follows H. H. Hobbs with the concession that those who fall away were Christians (Draper) who once had a "genuine spiritual experience" (Hobbs). They are still saved, according to these two former Presidents of the Southern Baptist Convention. Apparently so as to protect the theory of "once-saved, always-saved," they argue that these Christians are punished by being saved without serving! This is absurd.

God's sons need an example or model. God as our Father has given us Jesus as the example by which we are to live and serve. We are to look to Jesus "the pioneer and perfector of our faith, who for the joy that was set before him endured the cross, despising the shame and is seated at the right hand of the throne of God" (12:2). The word translated pioneer is *archēgos*, the word used in 2:10 after he has said that the one superior to the angels was "made lower than the angels, crowned with glory and honor because by the suffering of death, so that by the grace of God he might taste death for every one" (2:9).

In seventeenth century England those humble Bible-believing people who believed that they should follow the example of Jesus in all things, especially in believers' baptism and things related to salvation, were called Baptists, but their insistence on the death of Jesus for all men in general, not just for some, gave them the name of General Baptists. *The History of the English General Baptists*, 2 volumes, by Adam Taylor, 1818, gives many examples of those who made Jesus their example and our example today. People like Andrew Fuller, in his famous book *The Gospel Worthy of All Acceptation* (1785), illustrate what a struggle it was for a Particular Baptist like William Carey's faithful supporters to attempt to modify the hyper-Calvinist straight jacket. Fuller struggled with such distinctions as saying the death of Jesus was sufficient for all, efficient for some. He also made a distinction between the revealed will of God and hidden will, but God revealed his hidden will in Christ, according to Ephesians 3.

It is no wonder that the truly great Charles Spurgeon said he was "a very bad Calvinist." (See A.

C. Underwood, *A History of the English Baptists*, London, 1947, p. 204).

A. T. Robertson says that the title Perfecter (*teleiōten*) was "apparently coined by the writer from *teleioō* as it has been found nowhere else." (*Word Pictures*, V, p. 433). It is also possible to translate *anti tes charas*, ("for the joy"), as "instead of the joy," (*New Oxford Annotated Bible*, p. 1466n.), and I think that is correct. His suffering displaces his joy. Being crucified was no joy. Here we reach the heart of Baptist theology for the General Baptists down to the General Baptists under Bonino Stinson centered around Evansville, Indiana after 1822. The compromise of the United Baptists in Kentucky with Calvinism, when the Separate Baptists merged with the Regular Baptists in 1801, was too creedal for this legendary leader who would "put on the arousements" at the very mention of Hebrews 2:9. (See Ollie Latch, *General Baptists*, The General Baptist Press, 1968, pp. 76-85). On many occasions I have been heard gladly by these General Baptists with whom I seldom differ. It is too bad that Southern Baptists have not opened their fellowship to these genuine people. It is not too late if we go by the sound exegesis of the Greek New Testament by such giants as A. T. Robertson with whom I also seldom differ.

God our Father is like a good father in the flesh, according to Proverbs 3:11 and following, who chastises and corrects his son (Heb 12:7-11). This point is so pronounced that Joseph Barnabas uses another for those who are not disciplined for their sins. They are *nothoi* in the Greek, illegitimate children, bastards in the Authorized (King James) Version. The purpose of the earthly father is to lead his son to imitate and share his holiness. That leads to one of the major passages on holiness in the New Testament (Heb 12:12-17).

> Therefore lift your drooping hands and strengthen your weak knees, and make straight paths for your feet, so that what is lame may not be put out of joint but rather be healed. Strive for peace with all men, and for the holiness without which no one will see the Lord. See to it that no one fail to obtain the grace of God; that no "root of bitterness" spring up and cause trouble, and by it the many become defiled; that no one be immoral or irreligious like Esau, who sold his birthright for a single meal. For you know that afterward, when he desired to inherit the blessing, he was rejected, for he found no chance to repent, though he sought it with tears.

Discipline heals the crippled souls who are tempted to drop out of the race (12:13). Discipline is intended to make peace as much as possible (12:14). Discipline is intended to avoid the failure to obtain the grace of God in the future and to uproot bitterness that may cause others to be defiled, a warning in the Septuagint translation of Deuteronomy 29:18.

Esau, in Genesis 25:29-34, is the fatal Old Testament example that they should not imitate by selling their spiritual "birthright for a single meal" (12:16). A. T. Robertson comments: "Esau is a tragic example of one who does a willful sin which allows no second chance (Heb 6:6; 10:26). The author presses the case of Esau as a warning to the Christian who were tempted to give up Christ" (*Word Pictures*, V. 418).

So we yawn and take another dogmatic slumber before we awake to pass another resolution against any who disturb us. Robertson is commenting on the three passages on irreversible apostasy in Hebrews. Martin

Luther wanted to drop Hebrews from the New Testament canon because of these three passages, but the great William Tyndale warned him not to do it. Tyndale's introduction to Hebrews in his English translation of 1534 is a gem, but gratitude for his insight was expressed by choking him to death in his cell and burning his body at the stake. My, how the churches often reward sound scholarship!

In the light of Hebrews 12:17 we should renounce the dogmatic cliché of "once-saved, always-saved" and put in its place the saying, "once an apostate always an apostate." Esau "was rejected for he found no chance to repent, though he sought it with tears" (12:17). That is the conclusion to be reached by Esau's example in Genesis 27:30-40.

God as Judge

This fifth exhortation shifts from God as Father to God as Judge in one of the most awesome passages in the Bible (12:18-29). As a small boy who had never read the many useful commentaries from John Calvin (1549) to Harold W. Attridge (1989), I felt the power of this part of the exhortation and warning. I had never heard of Rudolf Otto and his wonderful analysis of experiences with God which he called the *mysterium tremendum et fascinans* (*The Idea of the Holy*, Galaxy, 1929), but I knew then that this was more than what a cynic called "spooky religion."

The very reading of the passage by Bill Day, the rustic pioneer preacher at the United Baptist Church of Jesus Christ at Lonesome Dove, Texas would cause me to look out the window of the oldest Baptist church in the Lone Star State. I would ponder the tombs of many of my ancestors just inside the gate of the cemetery and

wonder if the hymn by Isaac Watts often sung about
marching to Zion and the Scripture that said, "you have
come to Mount Zion" (12:22) really meant that the legendary leaders of the church who at one time sat on the
pews while the preachers with the King James Bible and
with their rifles and pistols at hand were really in the
Unseen Company even though their bodies had been
buried in the ground. I believed then and I believe now
that they were in the Unseen Choir and in the gathered
congregation. It is still good to hear the words and find
such writers as F. F. Bruce, my favorite expositor, who
in 1964 vindicated my interpretations while many found
the exhortation disturbing and dodged its almost obvious meaning. It made them uneasy, especially when
the possibility of accountability for their conduct and
for friends and family members flashed in their minds.
Our way of living can indeed make the words a comfort
in sorrow or a conviction of sin.

The description of Israel at Mount Sinai in Exodus
19:2 and following and Exodus 20:18-21 as background
reminds me of a personal experience when I climbed to
the traditional place where Moses experienced this
theophany. On the way up between St. Catherine's
Monastery near Elijah's cave, a snowstorm struck that
was so terrible that my wife Mildred and some other
women went back with a guide while I pressed on
above the storm to the top. It was beautiful beyond the
storm. On the way down, all alone, I decided to de-
scend through the traditional cleft in the rock mentioned later in the very old account in Exodus 33:22
where it is said, in the Authorized (King James) Version,
the Lord promised Moses would see his "hind parts"
(33:23). I am persuaded that this tradition is true and
that the traditional place is perhaps true, but my ex-

perience there in a thunder and lightning storm helps me to appreciate. The thunder roared and the lightning flashed much like James Weldon Johnson described it in his Creation poem (*God's Trombones*, Viking Press, 1965, p. 18). I pity those who are unable to appreciate such symbolism and the sense of the awesome.

The point made here by the author is that there is a "communion of saints," as many if not most Christians confess to believe. I do. In this communion we have "come to Mount Zion and to the City of the Living God, the heavenly Jerusalem, and to innumerable angels in festal gathering, and to the assembly of the first-born who are enrolled in heaven, and to a judge who is God of all, and to the spirits of just men made perfect, and to Jesus, the mediator of a new covenant, and to the sprinkled blood that speaks more graciously than the blood of Abel" (12:22-24).

There is general agreement with F. F. Bruce in the Calvinist commentaries that this is what the Westminster Shorter Catechism means in the Answer to Question 37: "The souls of believers are at their death made perfect in holiness, and do immediately pass into glory; and their bodies, being still united to Christ, do rest in their graves, 'til the Resurrection." Those in the soul-sleeping tradition of some Anabaptists and Martin Luther would postpone perfection for the redeemed until the resurrection. Still others, in the more Catholic and Anglican tradition, including myself, would be inclined toward a progressive perfection between death and resurrection. This is certainly the view in the Apocryphal writing of 2 Esdras which has a detailed statement of this progress in Paradise where there are degrees of blessedness for the righteous and the degrees of punishment in Hades for the wicked (chapter 7). Luther feared that this passage supported the Catholic doctrine of Purgatory so he threw 2 Edras into the Elba River.

John Calvin avoided the doctrine of a purgatory by his theory of an instant perfection at death rather than at the resurrection. That makes Calvin's book against soul-sleeping (*Psychopannycia*, 1534, 36, 42), his first theological writing, one of the most interesting documents of the Protestant Reformation. (Cf. William Blake, *Calvin and the Anabaptist Radicals*, Eerdmans, 1983, p. 26.) I think both Luther and Calvin have closed the discussion about progressive glorification in Paradise and progressive punishment in Hades too soon. The Baptist Faith and Message postpones glorification to the resurrection, but 2 Corinthians 3:18 clearly teaches progressive glorification even in this life. Why should not glorification continue between death and resurrection as in 2 Esdras 7?

With the two mountains of Sinai and Zion in the background this fifth exhortation brings the warning to a climax with the two voices (12:25-29), the one from earth and the other from heaven. The voice on earth shook the earth, but the one from heaven "not only the earth, but also heaven" as predicted in Haggai 2:6. Only the kingdom of God will remain unshaken. "Therefore let us be grateful for receiving a kingdom that cannot be shaken, and thus let us offer to God acceptable worship, with reverence and awe; for our God is a consuming fire" (12:28f.).

"God as a consuming fire" has been used as the title for the most comprehensive study on the biblical basis for belief in the conditional immortality of man. Hardly a passage in Scriptures is missed and most of the historical studies have been interpreted and evaluated by E. W. Fudge in his recent publication, *The Fire that Consumes* (Providential Press, 1982). Since both my book on *The Hope of Glory* (Eerdmans, 1964) and *The Word of Truth* (Eerdmans, 1981, 1990) took basically the same view, let me urge the reader to test the two historical alternatives of eternal torment and the universal salvation of all mankind against what seems to be a rather flawless statement which was formally condemned by the Roman Catholic Church at the Fifth Lateran Council in 1513. Most Calvinists have also condemned the view with the charge of annihilation pronounced with a hissing sound, down to this day. Actually, conditional immortality differs from the theory of annihilationism and the universalism of most of the Greek and Eastern theology and the Latin and Western theology on the basis of biblical theology. Biblical theology knows nothing of belief in the natural immortality of the soul that undergirds all of the three alternatives usually stated in standard textbooks.

This rejection of the natural immortality of the soul and the logical conclusion of that immortality as a gift of God to mortal man by grace through faith has been elaborated since Edward White, a Congregationalist minister, made it clear in his book on the life of Christ (1846, 1875).

A Baptist theology stating the difference between the theory of annihilationsm, which argued for a second chance at the resurrection of the dead, was clearly and calmly set forth by the Baptist Theologian, William Newton Clarke, in *An Outline of Christian Theology*, first published in 1889 (pp. 448-453). At the time of Clarke's classic book the standard for Baptist Calvinism was A. H. Strong's *Systematic Theology* (Judson Press, 1907), a Baptist adaptation of the Princeton Presbyterian Theology of Charles Hodge (1871-73). Most found it expedient to follow what was recently eulogized by David Wells as "the Stout and Persistent Theology of Charles Hodge" (*Christianity Today*, Vol. XVIII, August 30, 1974, p. 15).

It was only a little over a decade after David Wells made his stout statement for the theology of Hodge and consequently Strong that he found himself in the midst of a debate with one who shifted from a fireball fundamentalist in defense of biblical inerrancy based on Hodge and Strong to a bold statement for conditional immortality, and that in the same *Christianity Today*.

Until 1972 Clark Pinnock had been the leader for a whole band of Paul Pressler's inerrantists who were being trained, especially at the New Orleans Baptist Theological Seminary. In 1972 the first sign that Clark Pinnock was far ahead of his band appeared when he boldly stated his belief in a view in the possibility of apostasy that I had defended since 1941. This was in his exposition on Galatians in a book called *Truth on Fire* (Baker, 1972).

I understand that he was fired at Trinity Evangelical Seminary, Deerfield, Illinois. He went from there to the strongly evangelical Regents College in Vancouver where echoes often were heard that he not only agreed with me on apostasy but also on conditional immortality.

On March 20, 1987, in the midst of the so-called biblical inerrancy debate, an article by Clark Pinnock called "Fire—Then Nothing" argued also that the theory of the natural immortality of the soul, based not on Scripture but on the Greek philosophy of Plato, was at the bottom of the traditional theory of the punishment of eternal torment. None other than David Wells was called upon to put out Pinnock's fire, but he sputtered

badly. It seems the time has come to consider the value
of such biblical and historical studies as that of *The Fire
that Consumes* by E. W. Fudge in 1982. That just could
take us back all the way to Deuteronomy 4:24 and
Hebrews 12:29 that declare that "our God is a consuming fire." I know of no passage in Scripture when
rightly studied in context and in depth that does not
agree with that view. It is the fire that needs to be
contemplated, not the firing of those who sincerely seek
to accept the Scriptures as their final authority in faith
for doctrine. That is far better than building bonfires
for those considered heretics who just could be among
the heroes of the faith — "of whom the world was not
worthy" (Heb 11:38).

Some day, by the grace of God, may all see the
truth in the words of Thomas Helwys to King James I of
England in *A Short Declaration of the Mistery of Iniquity*
(1612): "Our lord the king is but dust and ashes as
we—though he should kill us we will speak the truth to
him" (p. 42).

This last quotation comes from the reprint edited
with a great introduction by the saintly and scholarly
H. Wheeler Robinson who has been my major model of
a true Baptist and great scholar of the Old Testament
(The Kingsgate Press, published by The Baptist Historical Society, 1935).

Let those who rant and pass mindless resolutions
read and realize what a real believer and an original
Baptist was in the beginning.